Malaysia

a travel adventure

photography by Bok Tai Siew

text by Lorien Holland

PERIPLUS

Contents

Published by Periplus Editions with editorial offices at
130 Joo Seng Road #06-01, Singapore 368357.

ISBN 0-7946-0406-4

Printed in Malaysia

Photo Credits
All photos by Bok Tai Siew except for the following: C. K. Ng:
pages 85 (below left and right), 91 (below), 94; S. G. Tan: page
107; A. T. Tang: page 52 (above); Ricky Teoh: pages 56 (below),
78 (below), 100, 102, 103 (above), 104 (below left).

Distributed by

Asia Pacific
Berkeley Books Pte Ltd
130 Joo Seng Road, #06-01, Singapore 368357
Tel: (65) 6280-1330; Fax (65) 6280-6290
inquiries@periplus.com.sg
www.periplus.com

Indonesia
PT Java Books Indonesia
Kawasan Industri Pulogadung
Jl. Rawa Gelam IV No. 9, Jakarta 13930
Tel: (62) 21 4682-1088; Fax: (62) 21 461-0207
cs@javabooks.co.id

Japan
Tuttle Publishing
Yaekari Building 3rd Floor, 5-4-12 Osaki
Shinagawa-ku, Tokyo 141 0032
Tel: (81) 3 5437-0171; Fax: (81) 3 5437-0755
tuttle-sales@gol.com

North America, Latin America & Europe
Tuttle Publishing
364 Innovation Drive, North Clarendon
VT 05759-9436, USA
Tel: 1 (802) 773-8930; Fax: 1 (802) 773-6993
info@tuttlepublishing.com
www.tuttlepublishing.com

Front endpaper: Chinese immigrants brought many traditions
with them to Malaysia, including female foot binding for richer
women in their community. Although foot binding is no longer
practised, replicas of the diminutive brocade shoes can still be
found in craft shops and museums.

Back endpaper: The fabulous façade of the Hui Kuan or Hokkien
Clan Association in Malacca.

Page 1: Dressed in traditional costume, this young woman
helps celebrate Malaysia's remarkable cultural diversity in its
annual "Citrawarna" (Colours of Malaysia) parade.

Page 2: Fireworks over the old Moorish-style law courts bor-
dering Dataran Merdeka (Independence Square) in downtown
Kuala Lumpur, heart of the colonial administration in Malaya.

Pages 4–5: Below left: A runner on the jogging track outside
the state-of-the-art Petronas Twin Towers in the Golden
Triangle business district of Kuala Lumpur. Below right: The
white sands and palm trees of Sipidan Water Village Resort
in the eastern state of Sabah are deliciously inviting. Top right:
All hotels and dive operators were evicted from the world-
renowned Sipidan dive site in 2005 in order to preserve its
unique environment, and divers are now accommodated in
romantic stilt villages like the Sipidan-Kapalai Resort. Right:
Until Malaysia's highway network got off the ground in the
1970s, Kuala Lumpur's old railway station, designed in Moorish
style by a British colonial architect, was the centre of activity.

Pages 6–7: Sunset on Penang's famous Batu Ferringhi Beach.

Malaysia: The Original Melting Pot

Long before New York became the melting pot of the New World, Malaysia was bubbling away, mixing cultures, religions and ways of life. From way back in the third century BC, when trading links were firmly established with China to the east and India to the west, Malaysia has been a fertile ground for the fusion of different faiths and ways of life. The result is a unique jumble of localized cultures involving aboriginals (Orang Asli), Malays, Chinese, Arabs, Sumatrans, Indians and Europeans, who have mingled and fought for control of trading rights and the country's rich natural resources.

Underneath that mesh of beliefs and religions, Malaysia is a humid, tropical landscape, where frangipani trees grow by the roadside, inviting white sands separate the land from the sea and the jungles are so dense that animal and plant species are still being discovered within. Encroaching on that landscape is, of course, a fast-expanding urban environment of office blocks, highways, billboards and shopping malls as the modern state of Malaysia reaches towards its goal of developed nation status by 2020.

I was quite unprepared for the degree of modernity in present-day Malaysia when I moved there in the year 2000. I had seen photographs of Kuala Lumpur's icon to progress, the Petronas Twin Towers. My sister, a long-term resident of the city, had also briefed me on the changes afoot. But the state-of-the-art airport, the modern highways, the swish hotels, the highly air-conditioned upmarket shopping centres – not to mention the traffic jams – were way beyond my expectations.

Until recent decades, Malaysia, or Malaya as it was called in colonial times, really was a backwater. Time passed slowly, palm oil, tin and rubber were the major industries, and people had time to sit and talk – as long as they were out of the sun and in the shade!

Still, the concept of time passing slowly should not be confused with time not passing at all. Malaysia has a very lengthy past. Human

remains dating back some 37,000 years have been found in the Niah Caves in eastern Malaysia. More recent ancestors moved southwards from China and Tibet around 10,000 years ago and make up the bulk of the indigenous populations of Orang Asli today. Later migrants brought fishing and sailing skills with them, and gave their name to the Malay Archipelago – lands which today make up the modern states of Malaysia, Indonesia, the Philippines, Singapore and Brunei.

Malaysia's geographical position at the crossroads between civilizations and trading routes meant outside influences were always strong, and often hard to resist. After the arrival of the Malays, there were four main waves of foreign influence and conquest, which eventually split the Malay Archipelago into separate political entities. This is not hard to understand when you see that Hindu India, the Islamic Middle East and Christian Europe lie to the west. To the northeast are Buddhist China and Japan; and the shipping routes linking them all pass right around modern Malaysia and through the Strait of Malacca.

The startling variety of food in Malaysia is a good illustration of these differing cultural streams. From the majority Malay population comes spicy coconut and lemon grass-based cuisine. Southern Indian, Hainanese, Cantonese, Hakka, Javanese, Sumatran, Middle Eastern and Portuguese foods all have large followings. There is even the celebrated Nyonya style, which is a mixture of Chinese and Malay cooking. And every so often you'll be offered a watery cucumber sandwich and a stiff cup of tea in a nod at British colonial rule.

The first major outside influence on the Malay-speaking world came from Indian and Chinese traders. The monsoon winds meant vessels had to pass down the east coast of Peninsular Malaysia, round the tip and past what is now Singapore, and up the other side through the Strait of Malacca. Indian influence was particularly strong, and old documents speak of Indian traders buying timber and jewels from the Malays.

By the first century AD, both Hinduism and Buddhism were well established in these coastal enclaves, and Chinese chronicles speak of a great port in the Strait of Malacca in the fifth century AD. Two hundred years later, the maritime kingdom of Srivijaya rose to strength, and controlled the coasts of Sumatra, Peninsular Malaysia and Borneo. The maharajahs of Srivijaya waxed and waned, but stayed in power for 700 years by controlling the spice trade through the region.

Records of the time are sparse, but a possible early capital currently under exploration is Kota Gelanggi, in the jungles of southern Malaysia near to Singapore. Other outposts were in northern Malaysia, while most of the kingdom was focused on Palembang on the north coast of Sumatra. Srivijaya came under increasing attack from others who wanted to tax the lucrative spice trade. The fatal blow came in the middle of the fourteenth century from the Hindu Majapahit empire from eastern Java.

This is really the point where today's Malaysian school children start their history lessons. A rebel prince called Parameswara escaped from Srivijaya when the empire fell and headed north, eventually establishing a coastal fiefdom around 1400. This was Malacca (Melaka in Malay), which quickly became the most important port in

Above: An aerial view of the heart of Kuala Lumpur. The large green rectangle is Independence Square, once the heart of the colonial administration when it was known as the Padang. The mock Tudor-style Selangor Club is on its left and the Sultan Abdul Samad Building on its right. The triangle of green is the confluence of Kuala Lumpur's two rivers and the point where the city started.

Right: The record-breaking Petronas Twin Towers are Malaysia's icon to modernity. Completed in 1998, they are eighty-eight stories high and were the world's tallest building until they were eclipsed by Taipei 101 in 2004. The skybridge which links the two towers is open to the public..

Below: The Kuala Lumpur Tower is the city's telecommunications beacon, complete with a revolving restaurant at its upper levels. It is built on top of a hill and appears to loom over the Petronas Twin Towers. Views over the city are unrivalled on a clear day.

Opposite: The National Monument is a larger than life-size bronze sculpture commemorating those who died in Malaysia's struggle for freedom, principally during the Japanese occupation in the Second World War and the 1948–60 Communist insurgency.

Southeast Asia, controlling the lands on both sides of the Malacca Strait and all the lucrative spice trade that passed through.

The port was the cultural lodestone of the archipelago, and when Parameswara converted from Hinduism to Islam in 1414, much of the region followed suit. What followed was the "golden age" of Malacca. The city deftly positioned itself to appeal to Indian, Chinese and Arab merchants, as well as all the local kingdoms. At the peak of its influence, some eighty languages were spoken in the city. To this day, the Malacca Sultanate is held up as the golden age of Malay self-rule.

But it was not to last. Tales of Malacca's wealth and influence reached as far as Venice and made the port a prime target for the expansionist Europeans. A Portuguese expedition sailed from India in 1511, and after a month-long siege took the city. The last Sultan escaped and moved the court south to Johor. The port of Malacca then went into a slow but terminal decline, because the Portuguese did not have the resources to force trade to continue at Malacca. Muslim traders, in particular, started to use the port of Aceh across the Strait in Sumatra.

Johor, too, rose in significance, and the ousted descendants of the Malacca Sultanate finally tasted revenge in 1641 when they helped the Dutch expel the Portuguese from Malacca. But they were not able to rid themselves of the Dutch, who took firm control of the lucrative spice trade.

More than a century later, the British started to close in on the spice trade, first by forcing the cession of the island of Penang in 1791, and then by starting a trading post on Singapore in 1819. The British and Dutch then divided the region between themselves in 1824, with Singapore, Malacca and Penang going to the British and the rest going to the Netherlands. The political border has stuck to this day, with Malaysia and Indonesia divided by the Strait of Malacca to the west and the island of Borneo to the east.

Malaysia is made up of a diverse collection of peoples and territories and makes a big deal of its diversity on National Day on 31 August each year. People dress in the national flag (far left), participate in musical and other routines (left) and parade in their regional costumes (below).

The armed forces and police take part in the National Day parade (above). Thousands of students, dressed in the colours of the Malaysian flag (right), also participate in choreographed formations reflecting the theme of the year's independence celebrations.

Borneo holds much sway in popular imagination as the land of the head-hunters, exotic animals and deep jungles. Until the seventeenth century, the entire island (it is the world's third largest) was ruled by the Brunei Sultanate. But increasing Dutch, Spanish and British control of the spice trade weakened the Sultan's grip on power. An English trader, James Brooke, became the "White Rajah" of the southwest of the island, and a British trading company held sway in the northwest. The east of the island fell under Dutch control. Somewhat remarkably, the Brunei Sultanate survived and remains an independent state, albeit as a tiny shadow of its former self.

Brunei retains close financial ties to Singapore, which joined Malaysia some years after its independence from Britain in 1957 but was then expelled from the union and is now also an independent state. The other two parts of western Borneo are a part of Malaysia, along with eleven states in Peninsular Malaysia.

Those eleven states consist of the old trading ports of Malacca and Penang and an amazing nine sultanates, which are a reminder of the days when small kingdoms proliferated all over the Malay Archipelago, and there was no overarching central power.

To avoid renewed rivalries between the nine Sultans, they elect a head of state from amongst their number every five years. The Yang di-Pertuan Agong, or King, of Malaysia does not hold enormous political power, but is the ceremonial ruler of the nation, and is held in very high regard. The King's palace in Kuala Lumpur, complete with red-jacketed guards on horseback, is very near my son's school. He often asks if he can go and play in the lovely gardens, but I tell him that his only hope is to write a very polite letter to the King, because the guards would never let him through the gates. They are defending their King and their independence as a sovereign state, and not even a small boy wanting to climb the fruit trees can go in without an invitation.

Left: Malaysia's ethnic Chinese community makes up around one-third of the population and is particularly noticeable in urban areas. The Chingay Festival in Penang is celebrated at the end of the year with dragon dances, as shown here, stilt walkers, acrobats, and decorated floats taking to the streets to the clashing of cymbals and the beating of gongs and drums.

Above: Chinese New Year is a big festival in Malaysia and is celebrated with traditional lion dances. The Chinese believe that having a lion dance troupe perform at their homes during Chinese New Year and at newly opened business premises will drive out evil spirits and usher in luck and prosperity. The acrobatics of the agile "lion" as it twists, climbs, hops and jumps from stilt to stilt to the beat of huge Chinese drums, is a memorable and colourful sight.

Left and Below: Much of the central part of Peninsular Malaysia is a protected reserve called Taman Negara, which stretches over 4343 sq km (1,683 sq miles). This contains some of the world's oldest jungles and is an excellent spot to experience the rainforest and see some of its diverse flora and fauna. Access is mainly by longboat (left), and attractions include an aerial walkway through the treetops (below right). The very lucky visitor might even spot a Malayan Tiger (below right), which appears on Malaysia's coat of arms and symbolizes strength and bravery. However, the Malayan Tiger is endangered, with less than a thousand animals left in the wild.

Right: Divers at Sipidan Island in eastern Sabah. Sipidan is Malaysia's top dive destination, and one of the world's best. More than 3,000 species of fish and several hundred coral species have been logged in its ecosystem.

Pages 24–5: A selection of Malaysian handicrafts involving basketry, metalwork and pottery at the Craft Complex in Kuala Lumpur.

Kuala Lumpur and the Hill Stations

Malaysia has several port cities with histories that stretch way back through the centuries. But its shiny bustling capital is not among them. To start with, Kuala Lumpur is not even on the coast, but inland near the mountains. Perhaps most remarkably, it is in a spot that was inhabited by jungle animals only 150 years ago.

Kuala Lumpur is a city that has come a long way very quickly. It is also a city that really explains Malaysia's recent past, from its absorption into the British Empire through to independence, the Communist insurgency and subsequent rapid economic growth.

The first people to set up camp on the site of modern-day Kuala Lumpur were migrant labourers from China. They travelled up the Klang River from the coast in 1857, in search of tin to mine, and they stopped at the confluence of the Klang and the Gombak rivers because the water became too muddy and shallow to navigate any further.

Of that group of eighty-seven prospectors, only eighteen survived malaria and other pestilences. But they persevered at the spot which they called Kuala Lumpur (it actually means "muddy confluence" in Malay) and eventually found lots and lots of tin. The Malay Sultans of the area, who lived in the royal town of Klang near the coast, had sanctioned the foray into the jungle in return for taxation on the tin. At first they were delighted with their new-found wealth. But civil war broke out in 1867 over control of the tin mines, and in 1872 one of the warring factions razed Kuala Lumpur to the ground. At this point the British, who were increasingly reliant on tin from Selangor, forced the Sultan of Selangor to accept a British Resident to "advise" on matters of governance.

Kuala Lumpur was rebuilt by the Chinese miners, more tin was discovered, and in 1880 Selangor moved its capital from Klang to Kuala Lumpur. The railway line to the coast opened in 1886, and in 1895 the British created the Federated Malay States from Selangor and three

Left: View through a Moorish arch of the Railway Administration Building to the old railway station of Kuala Lumpur.

Above: Dancers in front of the Sultan Ahmad Samad Building during the "Colours of Malaysia" parade.

Top: The copper domes of the Sultan Ahmad Samad Building are now dwarfed by encroaching skyscrapers and modernity. But the building was once the centre of the colonial administration of Malaya, and the grass in the foreground used to be a cricket pitch.

Pages 26–7: Kuala Lumpur's Golden Triangle business district at sunset, with the iconic Petronas Twin Towers in the centre. The skyscrapers and infrastructure in the area are less than fifty years old, and have eclipsed the old town centre to the south.

other neighbouring Sultanates. Booming Kuala Lumpur naturally became the capital.

By this stage Kuala Lumpur was a melting pot of different peoples, none of whom could claim to own the city outright. The native Malays came from differing parts of the peninsula and Sumatra. The Chinese were largely economic migrants from the south of China, and there was also a sizeable Indian population made up of colonial administrators and rubber estate workers who had been drafted in by the British.

The town was still small, but it had its distinct Malay, Chinese, Indian and British colonial zones, which remain to this day and are a good starting point for getting a grip on the city. Perhaps the best place to start is the Masjid Jamek, a romantic Moorish-style mosque that was designed by the resident colonial architect in 1907 for the Malay community. This mosque is on the spur of land at the confluence of the two rivers where the Chinese tin prospectors landed in 1857. It is the historical heart of Kuala Lumpur. Visitors are welcome any time except prayer time (when it gets very crowded with worshippers) and the cool marble colonnades

and palm trees are a welcome respite from the heat of the city. Although the two rivers which run down either side of the mosque and converge below it are now in deep concrete channels to prevent flooding, the site retains an exotic charm.

Standing at this convergence of the rivers, the original town spreads out in all directions. To the west are the law courts and the centre of the British colonial administration, complete with club, church and cricket pitch, and the peaceful Lake Gardens unfolding on the hills beyond. To the east are the temples and hustle and bustle of Chinatown, where chicken rice is a staple (and delicious) lunch. Directly north is Little India, which is the centre of north Indian Muslim culture in Kuala Lumpur, and a good spot to grab a fresh *naan* bread and *dahl*. In the early days, Little India was actually a Malay settlement, but most Malays moved about a mile further north to Kampong Baru (which means New Village in Malay) after land was opened up for them in 1899.

Kampong Baru is an interesting case study in Malaysian politics. The land was designated

Berlepas
Departure

↑

Dalam Negeri
Domestic

↑

Antarabangsa
International

Above: The main terminal and control tower at the futuristic Kuala Lumpur International Airport, popularly referred to as KLIA, which was opened in 1998 and has the expansion space and runway capacity for the next generation of super jumbo jets.

Right: The national carrier, Malaysia Airlines, uses for its logo the Malay moon kite (*wau bulan*), so-called because of its crescent-shaped tail, popular in the eastern states of Kelantan and Terengganu.

Right: Kuala Lumpur International Airport is routinely voted one of the world's best airports for is calm, open spaces, great shopping and ease of use.

Above: Suria KLCC (Kuala Lumpur City Centre) contains six floors of shopping heaven and prides itself as being at the centre of slick, modern Malaysia. For those not too keen on shopping, there are lots of restaurants, a multi-screen cinema and a great interactive museum called Petrosains.

Right: Luxury goods and even winter wear (which is rarely needed in Kuala Lumpur's balmy climate) for sale in Suria KLCC.

Opposite: Suria KLCC is right under the Petronas Twin Towers, and looks over a beautifully landscaped park and playground that was once Kuala Lumpur's racecourse.

as Malay Agricultural Land back in 1899, in order to encourage food production and ensure the Malays were not disenfranchised by the far more business-minded Chinese. Of course, Kuala Lumpur has expanded well beyond Kampong Baru, which is now in the heart of the city, only a stone's throw away from the monumental Petronas Twin Towers and the surrounding Golden Triangle business district. While this area has developed fast and furiously, with glittering architecture and a forest of high rises, Kampong Baru has stood still. The old wooden houses, the night market, the village feel are all still there. This little oasis is a great place to eat some Malay favourite foods like *nasi lemak*.

If you don't fancy a sweaty walk around these historically distinct zones, then the lofty Kuala Lumpur Tower offers a good view down on them all. This is a telecommunications tower with a revolving restaurant at the top, so as you enjoy your food you can gaze out at old Kuala Lumpur and also see the extent of the city's new suburbs. Great scars of red earth on distant hills are evidence of yet more construction, and the large number of lakes dotted around the place

are the flooded remains of the open tin mines that brought the city its wealth and fame.

On a clear day, you can see the highways slinking south past the new administrative capital of Putrajaya and out towards the futuristic Kuala Lumpur International Airport (KLIA). Putrajaya is a purpose-built city that houses most of Malaysia's ministries and law courts and is rising out of old palm oil plantations. At present, both Putrajaya and the airport seem impossibly far from Kuala Lumpur itself, but the palm oil plantations that still occupy much of the 32 kilometre (20 mile) distance between the two are fast disappearing into housing and industrial estates. In a few decades, it will be one enormous urban corridor.

In fact, the only large swathes of greenery you will see from the Kuala Lumpur Tower are on the densely forested hills to the north. These rise into the Titiwangsa Range, which is the backbone of the peninsula. One enterprising Malaysian Chinese has built an entire resort up on this mountain range, at a height of 1800 metres (6,000 feet) above sea level. It took four years to build the access road, and many more to expand the resort to its current enormous size. At such a height, the weather is refreshingly cool and a welcome respite from the heat of Kuala Lumpur. But the main attractions of the

Genting Highlands are its gambling halls and amusement park.

Further afield, the colonial-era hill stations of Fraser's Hill and the Cameron Highlands still maintain a little of their Old World charm, complete with slightly damp furnishings and half-timber Tudor-style bungalows. These hill stations advertise themselves as "little England", but they are far more exotic than that, and even in the neatly planted tea plantations, the chaos of the jungle is never very far away. Gibbons call to each other across the valleys and leeches are almost inevitable. In fact, the whole hill station environment must be reminiscent of Kuala Lumpur in its early days, when the balance between man and nature was clearly in nature's favour. Of course, concrete and tarmac now have a formidable upper hand in Kuala Lumpur, and the sounds of the jungle have been usurped by ever-expanding road traffic. You will quickly discover that peak-time traffic jams can be horrendous, but there is a monorail line and an underground train system which are easy to navigate. And wherever you go, you cannot help but remark on the capital's extraordinary diversity, from food to dress to architecture and places of worship. It is not hard to see how the tourism board came up with the slogan "Malaysia, truly Asia."

Opposite: The Federal Highway, a major artery connecting central Kuala Lumpur with the urban sprawl of nearby Petaling Jaya.

Above: The automated Putra Light Rail Transit (LRT) connects Kuala Lumpur's eastern and western suburbs. In the centre of town, the line runs underneath the Petronas Twin Towers and the central business district and comes up above street level in Chinatown.

Left: The monorail is the latest addition to Kuala Lumpur's public transport network. It zigzags through the Golden Triangle centre of town and ends up at KL Sentral, the new transit hub for the city that brings together the commuter, intercity and airport express rail networks with Kuala Lumpur's light rail transit system.

Above: Fruit stalls at the Petaling Street night market in Kuala Lumpur's Chinatown, selling local rambutans, mangosteens and mangoes, alongside imported apples.

Right: Traditional Malaysian cakes are largely made with rice flour and coconut and come in a great variety of colours and textures.

Top: This pancake-like food is *murtabak*, an Indian Muslim dish. The filling is usually fried mutton with onion, garlic and cucumber, and the best place to try one is on a streetside food stall.

Above: These small beef and chicken kebabs are called *satay*, and are popular all over Southeast Asia. Malaysia Airlines has adopted *satay* as its signature food to cook on the spot and serve to first-class passengers.

Right: *Teh tarik* (literally "pulled tea") is a stalwart of the Malaysian coffee shop. It is made from well-brewed tea and condensed milk which is passed back and forth between two large mugs until it is frothy.

The Sin Sze Si Ya Temple is the oldest temple in Chinatown, and in Kuala Lumpur's formative years was the focal point for the ethnic Chinese community. First built in 1864, the temple is unique in that the two main deities worshipped here are not traditional deities from China, but two community leaders who died in the chaotic early days of tin mining in Malaysia. The unusual angles of the temple's arches, walls and staircases result from an orientation based on *feng shui* principles. Its ornate interior and elaborate roof ridges make it one of the finest examples of traditional Chinese temple architecture in Malaysia.

Above, right and opposite:
Hindus celebrate Thaipusam in January or February each year, and the Batu Caves in the outskirts of Kuala Lumpur are arguably the world's biggest focal point for Thaipusam celebrations. Participants shave their heads and undertake a series of devotions along a pilgrimage route to the caves. Most carry burdens such as a pot of coconut milk. But many enter a trance and pierce their skin with up to 108 metal skewers to intensify their penance. They then climb up the 272 steps into the cave, with its shrines to Lord Murugan, the youngest son of Shiva and Parvati.

Southeast Asia's fastest moving cable car takes passengers up to the Genting Highlands, a massive resort with over 8,000 hotel rooms which is on the Titiwangsa Range to the north of Kuala Lumpur. The Genting Highlands are only an hour from Kuala Lumpur, but are an impressive 1800 m (6,000 ft) above sea level so the weather is refreshingly cool and misty. Most people go there to play in its extensive theme park and entertainment centre, attend conventions or gamble. As Genting is the only licensed casino in the country, it is often called the Las Vegas of Malaysia.

Above: Fraser's Hill also sits on the heights of the Titiwangsa Range, a little further away from Kuala Lumpur than the Genting Highlands, but is a whole world apart. It does not have cable cars or glitzy entertainment, but instead retains much of its Old World charm. Visitors can stay in the oldest stone bungalows in Malaysia. It is also a favourite spot for ornithologists.

Left: An Orang Asli, or aboriginal, hunter from the Cameron Highlands demonstrating the use of a blowpipe.

Left and below: The Cameron Highlands are the most beautiful and extensive of Malaysia's hill stations. Even though they are a good three-hour drive from Kuala Lumpur, there has been a recent spate of rapid development that has destroyed some of their charm. Nevertheless, the Cameron Highlands are an enchanting spot to have a round of golf (left), gaze out over the tea estates (below) planted during the colonial era, visit the many flower and vegetable farms, or simply sit and enjoy a cup of your favourite English tea and a plate of freshly baked scones.

Penang and Langkawi: The Western Islands

The tropical islands of Penang and Langkawi are both in the Malacca Strait, off the west coast of Malaysia. They are among Malaysia's top tourist destinations and were once both controlled by an ancient Hindu kingdom which traded with Sri Lanka and the Indian subcontinent.

Beyond that, their histories diverge significantly. Penang was a British possession from 1786, and became a great trading city, the "Pearl of the Orient". It still has the third largest economy in Malaysia, after Kuala Lumpur and Johor. Langkawi, on the other hand, has remained a rural backwater and hiding place for pirates for most of its modern history. Tourism only took off on the island a few decades ago, and it still retains much of its laid-back bucolic charm.

The ferry between the two islands takes just under three hours, making them a great double destination to first soak up a bit of Straits Settlements history and then head for the beach. Both are favourite destinations for Europeans, especially during the winter.

Of course, the first Europeans in the region were not looking for holiday spots, but a place to make a foothold in the lucrative spice trade which ran through the Malacca Strait. First the Portuguese and then the Dutch had taken control of the port of Malacca, further to the south. When Francis Light arrived on Penang Island in 1786 with the plan of opening a free port for the East India Company, there had been Europeans in the region for more than 150 years.

Light came to an agreement with the Sultan of Kedah to cede Penang in exchange for protecting Kedah against the Siamese. But when the Siamese attacked, the Sultan of Kedah got no assistance from Light. He tried to retake the island in 1790 but eventually settled for a yearly payment of 6,000 Spanish dollars. By that stage, Penang already had 5,000 residents who were attracted to the free port and the chance to own any land they cleared. When Light died of malaria four years later, he left a son who went on to establish the Australian city of Adelaide,

Page 50: A sparkling view from Penang Hill of the lights of George Town, with the sixty-five storey Komtar Building in the foreground and the mainland town of Butterworth in the distance.

Page 51: The Penang Bridge, completed in 1985, connects the island of Penang to the mainland. At 13.5 km (8 miles), it is one of the world's longest bridges.

Left: The Kapitan Kling Mosque in George Town, which was built by Indian Muslim traders from the Coromandel Coast in the early nineteenth century.

Below: George Town City Hall, built in 1903, was one of the first buildings in Penang to be completely fitted with electric lights and ceiling fans. Penang's municipal council now uses the building for high-level meetings.

and a thriving entrepôt of traders in the new township of George Town on Penang. The island started accumulating serious wealth and status as a staging post for the East India Company's opium trade between India and China. Other important commodities that were traded through the port were pepper, cloves, nutmeg, tin and later rubber.

Traders and settlers came from mainland Malaysia, China, Sumatra, the Indian subcontinent, Thailand, Burma, the Arab world and Europe, and the street names today (Armenian Street and Rangoon Road, for example) reflect that diversity. Penang's food also reflects its great smattering of different cultural influences and is arguably the best in Malaysia. While foreigners tend to go to the beaches and sights of Penang, most locals go there primarily to eat.

In 1819, one of Penang's former administrators, Stamford Raffles, went south and established Singapore. This was to have a big impact on Penang, as Singapore completed the trio of British Straits Settlements down the Malacca Strait and eventually went on to eclipse Penang in importance. Still, Penang thrived through the nineteenth century and the early twentieth century. Some of its eminent visitors were Somerset

Maugham, Zhou Enlai, Joseph Conrad, Rudyard Kipling, Jawaharlal Nehru and Herman Hesse. Many of them stayed at Penang's best hotel, the Eastern and Oriental, which used to advertise itself as the "premier hotel east of Suez", and was owned by the same family that built the Raffles in Singapore and the Strand in Rangoon.

Penang had, and still has, a majority ethnic Chinese population. When the Japanese invaded the island at the end of 1941, shortly after bombing the American fleet at Pearl Harbor, they saw the Chinese as the enemy (because of ongoing hostilities with mainland China). They treated them with great brutality and some 40,000 ethnic Chinese across the Straits Settlements and Malaya were killed in horrific cleansing programmes. These atrocities, coupled with the fact that the British administration had fled and left the people of Penang to defend themselves against the Japanese, meant that things were irrevocably changed when Japan surrendered and Britain took back the island in 1945.

The Straits Settlements were dissolved in 1946 and Penang became part of the Federation of Malaya, and later Malaysia. Penang remains the only state in Malaysia which has a majority of ethnic Chinese. Although it has maintained

Above: Wat Chayamangkalaram houses the world's third longest reclining Buddha at 32 m (105 ft) and is the centre of the Thai community in Penang. Statues of serpentine creatures coil along the pathway leading to the entrance, which is guarded by mythical Thai "birdmen".

its economic strength with a large electronics and semiconductor production base, there have been many protests of late that the island is slipping backwards and needs to be restored to its former glory.

Whatever the perceived inequities, Penang is still an enchanted place to visit. Much of the old city of George Town remains, and the Penang Heritage Trust runs some excellent tours around the more interesting streets. Love Lane is a charming little distraction, while the Khoo Kongsi clan house, with its ornate mythical figures and blue dragons, contrasts well with nearby St. Georges Church, an elegant Palladian-style construction. Suffolk House, the grandiose residence of Light and early governors of Penang, is under a lengthy restoration which started in 2000, and is occasionally open to visits. The fantastic Cheong Fatt Tze Mansion, once home of the "Rockefeller of the East", is open every day and you can also stay the night.

High above George Town is Penang Hill, the first of the colonial hill stations built by the British. At 800 metres (2,600 feet) above sea level, it is remarkably cool and breezy, and has a number of government rest houses, the Bellevue Hotel and a defunct sanitarium for exhausted colonial officials. There are also several private houses perching on the steep slopes.

Penang's best beaches are on the north of the island and are rather built up with long concrete strips of hotels. Certainly, they pack in the crowds and get a lot of repeat business, but for my money Langkawi offers a better beach experience and remains reasonably undeveloped.

Langkawi and its surrounding 103 islets are just south of the border with Thailand, and for several periods in history were under Siamese control. Most recently, the island and the entire Sultanate of Kedah was handed over to Thailand by the Japanese during the Second World War.

Langkawi has been seriously off the beaten track for several centuries. One legend talks of a curse on the island that lasted seven genera-

tions and only ended in recent decades. In fact, only in 1987 did the island get tax-free status for the purpose of developing tourism, and serious construction started on the paddy fields. Now it is home to several uber-luxurious hotels and lots of friendly little places on the beach. Perhaps one of the most remarkable places is Bon Ton, which collected old wooden village houses from across the island and converted them into stylish rooms for holiday-makers.

As befits such a bucolic paradise, Langkawi still has lots of legends to explain the position of its mountains and the way that rivers flow. Perhaps the most intriguing story is of the Lake of the Pregnant Maiden. This is a freshwater lake on one of the outlying islands. Legend has it that a fairy once married an earthly Langkawi prince. Their first child died shortly after birth, and the distraught fairy buried the baby in the crystal clear waters of the lake. She left the mortal world and returned to her fairy bower, but first blessed the lake so that women who bathe in its waters will conceive. Whatever, it is a delightful spot for a swim and doing what Langkawi does best – relaxing in the sun.

Above: The indigo blue outer walls of the rambling Cheong Fatt Tze Mansion in George Town, a Chinese courtyard house built at the end of the nineteenth century. Inside are five courtyards, thirty-eight rooms and a fascinating mix of Chinese and British architectural detail.

Left: A snake charmer demonstrating his traditional routine at the Cheong Fatt Tze Mansion during the Penang Festival, held annually in December.

Right: A paragliding tourist coming into land on Batu Ferringhi Beach in Penang.

Within Malaysia, Penang is most famous for its food (top) which comes in a wide spectrum of styles and reflects the island's multicultural character. Mangosteens (left) are known as the "Queen of Fruits". Their tangerine-like segments are creamy with a touch of peach flavour, and are incredibly moreish. *Ais kacang* (above) is more of an acquired taste. Sweet corn, red beans and grass jelly are topped with shaved ice, colourful syrups and evaporated milk.

Penang's hawker centre on Gurney Drive is the best place to start feasting like the locals. Dishes range from the humble fried noodle (far left) to more upmarket steamed crab (left). A particular favourite is *laksa*, a bowl of steamed rice vermicelli generously garnished with finely sliced vegetables and covered with a steaming hot fish curry soup.

Above and right: Langkawi boasts some of the best beaches and laid-back attitudes in Malaysia. Sunsets framed by a sprinkling of Langkawi's 103 outlying islets are spectacular (above) while even the larger developments, like the 502-room Berjaya Langkawi Resort and Spa (right), have great empty expanses of beach – particularly in the middle of the day.

Malacca: Historic Trading Centre

Malacca is the historical heart of Malaysia and the basis of its modern federation of sultanates. While bustling new Kuala Lumpur looks forward, sleepy old Malacca looks backwards, towards its golden age of self-rule and supremacy in the global spice trade. In those days, its fame stretched as far as Venice and its territories into modern-day Indonesia and Singapore.

That all ended rather abruptly when Portugal lay siege to the bustling port of 50,000 inhabitants in 1511. Portugal went on to establish the first European colony in Southeast Asia at Malacca. After that, the influence of the port went into a very slow but steady decline, as Malacca spent almost 150 years under Portuguese control, then fell under Dutch and finally British rule. Perhaps its most recent moment of glory was in 1956 when Malaysia's first prime minister announced in Malacca that he had agreement with London and independence would soon be achieved. Independence the following year marked the end of more than four centuries of foreign control for Malacca.

One of the advantages of Malacca's slow removal from mainstream history is that much of its Portuguese and Dutch centre was preserved, rather than cleared for development, making it a great place to visit if you are at all interested in colonial history. However, modern Malacca has not done all it could to preserve its historical assets. A land reclamation project on the river front and rather haphazard application of planning rules means that the port has still not achieved UNESCO World Heritage status, although there are hopes that it will come soon, in a joint listing with Penang.

The Malacca Sultanate reached the peak of its supremacy in the middle of the fifteenth century. Its power reached into Sumatra, across the entire Malay Peninsula and over to Borneo. It attracted hundreds of ships each year, trading nutmeg and cloves from the Molucca Islands, pepper from Sumatra, tin and rattan from Peninsular Malaysia, camphor from Borneo, silk and

Above: St. Paul's Church dates from 1521. It was built by the Portuguese, and used by the Dutch after they took the city. It fell into disrepair after 1760. and when the British took control in 1824 they used it as a gunpowder store. The church walls still remain and fine old granite tombstones stand around the interior.

Left: The Porta de Santiago is one of the oldest surviving remnants of European architecture in Asia. It was once part of the much larger A'Famosa Fort, built by the Portuguese after they captured Malacca in 1511.

Page 62: The Malacca River, once a hive of trading activity, is now a sleepy waterway and its vessels are involved in the tourist trade rather than the spice trade.

Above: The multi-gabled Malacca Sultanate Palace is a replica of the original wooden palace that stood in the city before the Portuguese invasion of 1511. It was constructed in the traditional way without nails following descriptions and references found in old Malay texts, and it houses a cultural museum.

Page 63: At the centre of Dutch Square is the Malacca Clock Tower, built by a wealthy Straits Chinese family in 1886, when Malacca was under British rule. The clock mechanism, imported from England, eventually gave out and was replaced by a Japanese clock in 1982.

porcelain from China, and textiles from India.

Malacca paid tribute to Ming China and enjoyed the patronage of Muslim traders. But the Sultanate was caught offguard by the Portuguese, who had taken Goa in India and had their sights on Malacca and the spice trade. In 1511, Portugal took the port after forty days of fighting and then quickly built the A'Famosa Fort to fight off the waves of counter attacks that were to follow. They also built a lighthouse and watch tower at Cape Rachardo, north of Malacca, that allowed them to control the Malacca Strait.

The Portuguese could not control all the territories that had belonged to the Sultanate, but they did encourage the inhabitants of Malacca – mainly Malays and Straits Chinese – to remain in the city. The Dutch did the same when they wrested control from Portugal in 1641, although they never placed much importance on Malacca, keeping most of their forces and administration at Batavia (modern-day Jakarta). When the British took over, they maintained first Penang and then Singapore as the capital of the Straits Settlements, with Malacca always playing second fiddle. During Japan's occupation in the Second World War, Malacca slipped further out of the mainstream when its railway line was dug up and sent to Burma.

Today, nothing save the two tombs of Malay warriors remains from the Malacca Sultanate, although a reproduction of the Sultan's wooden palace stands in the city centre, near to the last remaining gateway of the A'Famosa fort. The Dutch Stadthuys and several churches, mosques and Chinese temples make for interesting visits, as does the old merchant quarter.

But perhaps the most remarkable part of Malacca is its population of Straits-born Chinese, or Peranakan ("born here"), many of whom can trace their history back to the early days of the Sultanate and have created a culture that mixes Malay and Chinese influences. Peranakan men (Babas) and women (Nyonyas) speak Malay interspersed with Chinese. They blend Malay spices with southern Chinese cooking, and have created the embroidered translucent *kebaya* blouse worn with a Malay batik sarong. Modernity has seen most Straits Chinese reabsorbed into mainstream Chinese culture, but they have left lots of reminders of their existence in Malacca.

Pages 66–7: The Stadthuys, or Town Hall, was built a decade after the Dutch seized Malacca in 1641. In 1753, the Dutch built Christ Church alongside it. Although the Clock Tower is painted the same red colour, and is at the centre of Dutch Square, it was added over a century later.

Left: Jonkers Street, now called Jalan Hang Jebat, leads away from Dutch Square and is lined with traditional shophouses dating back to the seventeenth century. Many of the shops now sell antiques and bric-a-brac. Restaurants serve the Malaccan dish of chicken rice balls.

Above: Trishaw drivers in central Malacca.

Top and right: The Cheng Hoon Teng Temple in downtown Malacca is the oldest Chinese temple in Malaysia, dating back to 1645, and is dedicated to the Goddess of Mercy.

Above: Interior of the Baba and Nyonya Heritage Museum showing the eclectic mix of style and architecture adopted by the ethnic Chinese who moved to Malaysia several centuries ago and married into the local community.

Left: Art Nouveau tiled steps in the Baba and Nyonya Heritage Museum, a former Straits Chinese townhouse built in 1896 in a style known as Chinese Palladian – a fusion of Chinese, Victorian and tropical architectural elements.

Opposite: The central light well in the Baba and Nyonya Heritage Museum gives a Portuguese feel to the courtyard, and provides light for the interior of this terraced house.

Above: The traditional shop-houses of Jalan Hang Kasturi have been restored and transformed into inviting restaurants and food stalls for the hungry visitor.

Left Façade of the Hotel Puri, the former residence of a wealthy Baba Nyonya family in Malacca. The family also paid for the construction of Malacca's Clock Tower.

Opposite: The Maritime Museum is housed inside a full-scale replica of a Portuguese vessel named *Flor de la Mar*, which sank without trace after it set sail from Malacca in 1511, laden with riches from the city.

Top: A typical village house in Malacca. The structure is raised off the ground and has a long covered verandah.

Left: Bullock carts in Malacca have pointed roofs in the shape of a bull's horn and other colourful trappings.

Above: Malay girls playing *congkat*, a tactical game using a board with two different types of holes, where the aim is to capture all your opponent's "seeds", which may be shells, marbles or stones.

Right: A curved staircase covered in colourful Art Nouveau tiles – a remnant of Malacca's cosmopolitan past – leads up to the house of a village headman at Melimbau on the outskirts of Malacca. The house, built in 1894, also has fine woodcarvings along its eaves.

Kelantan and Terengganu: The Malay Heartlands

Most of Malaysia is rushing headlong into modernity. But the northeastern states of Kelantan and Terengganu have taken a more relaxed approach to development, and in their deliberate, slow advance have kept much of traditional Malay culture alive.

The people who live in these states are almost entirely Malay. There are very few of the ethnic Chinese, Indian and other peoples who make up such a vibrant part of Malaysia's big cities. Even the few Chinese who do live in Kelantan and Terengganu are highly integrated into society. The result is a hospitable, largely rural society, where Islam is the uncontested religion, the weekend runs Friday to Saturday, road signs are in traditional Jawi script, and Malay arts and crafts like batik, kite making and top spinning are widely practised.

Kelantan, and to a lesser extent, Terengganu, have always felt separate from the rest of Peninsular Malaysia. For a start, the Titiwangsa Range makes transportation tricky from the west coast. Even today, a road trip from Kuala Lumpur to Kota Bharu (the state capital of Kelantan) takes more than eight hours. Moreover, the two states have never felt a particularly strong political affiliation to other parts of Malaysia. For long periods they were vassal states of Siam, and were closely connected to the Malay Sultanate of Patani in what is now southern Thailand. The Kelantanese dialect of Malay, which other Malaysians find hard to understand, is heavily influenced by the Thai language, and the Kelantanese royal family maintains strong connections to the Thai royals. For the most part, the Kelantanese border with Thailand is nothing more than a narrow river. Children cross the border to go to school, and until the recent upsurge in separatist violence in southern Thailand, there was continuous traffic across the border.

Kelantan and Terengganu were early trading ports by virtue of their position on the South China Sea. They were probably the first parts of Malaysia to convert to Islam, as evidenced by

Pages 76–7: The idyllic beach at the Perhentian Island Resort, nestled on a private palm-fringed cove at the largest island among the Perhentian group, off the coast of Terengganu. Coral reefs lie just off-shore and small fish come and nibble your toes if you sit in the shallow water.

Above: Pantai Dasar Sabak is one of the few remaining traditional fishing villages in Malaysia and is famous for its painted boats. It was the point where Japanese forces landed in 1941, before moving southwards to Singapore.

the Terengganu Stone, which is a granite block dating to AD 1326 and inscribed with Islamic law in Sanskrit, Malay and Arabic.

In both states, a conservative form of Islam is still practised. Public displays of affection are frowned upon, alcohol is restricted and women are expected to dress modestly. At the same time, the women of Kelantan have a nationwide reputation as fierce and competent business people, who control the family purse strings. One of the best places to see them in action is the Central Market in Kota Bharu, where they trade in fruits, vegetables, nuts and cakes. They also trade most of the batik made in the area.

Traditional top spinning and kite flying tend to be more of a male preserve. The tops are heavy wood and metal plates. Top spinning competitions are common activities between neighbouring villages, but for the visitor, the Kelantan Cultural Centre in Kota Bharu is probably the best place to go to catch a spin or two. Naturally, kites flying high in the sky are easier to spot than a spinning top, and are flown all over the area, especially after harvest time. Malay kites have an interesting history dating

back to the Malacca Sultanate in the sixteenth century, and are made of bamboo and paper. The most common design is a crescent moon kite (*wau bulan*), which is also used as the logo for Malaysia Airlines.

Wayang Kulit, or shadow puppet plays, are a slightly more contentious part of East Coast culture. The conservative leadership in Kelantan tried to ban them in the late twentieth century because many of the stories continued to be Hindu-based epics, and not Islamic. At the same time, interest in this centuries-old art was waning. But of recent years, there has been a small revival, partly because the Kelantan leadership relaxed its ban after coming close to losing the state election in 2004.

Culture aside, one of the main pulls of the east coast is its fabulous beaches and diving. Near to Kota Bharu, modesty is definitely the key. The authorities even changed the name of a stretch of sand from Pantai Cinta Berahi (Beach of Passionate Love) to the more sedate Pantai Cahaya Bulan (Moonlight Beach). Religious views are a little more relaxed on the outlying islands, making places like the Perhentian Islands and Redang Island popular destinations for those in search of a beach holiday. Certainly, the diving

and beaches are second to none, but the area is affected by the northeast monsoon and weather between November and March can be patchy.

South of Kota Bharu is Kuala Terengganu, the state capital of Terengganu. Despite its historical ties to the states of Johor, Malacca and Siam, and its one-time rule over neighbouring Kelantan, the town does not have as much charm as Kota Bharu. Many of its wooden buildings have been replaced with concrete blocks, and its traditional boat building industry has largely collapsed. However, revenues from large petroleum finds off the coast promise to change the situation, and there is renewed talk of a highway which would link into the national network and make Kuala Terengganu more accessible. For now, large petroleum installations around Dungun in the south of the state are about the only interruption to a great succession of coastal villages with their raised houses, swaying coconut palms and tin-roofed mosques. But I would recommend visiting sooner rather than later, because modernity is approaching fast. And the things that visitors like to see – old wooden stilt houses, unsealed roads and very little industry – are exactly what most locals would like to change.

Above: Divers heading towards traditional fishing vessels converted into passenger boats for a trip across the South China Sea to the Perhentian Islands.

Opposite: Redang Island is one of nine islands off the coast of Terengganu which make up a fantastic marine park. A colourful array of marine life and coral gardens make for great snorkelling and scuba diving.

Left: Women are big traders in Kelantan, and their formidable presence is best felt in Kota Bharu's Central Market, where they dominate the fresh food business.

Right: A Kelantanese woman wearing a traditional folded batik headcloth winnowing rice in a paddy field. Kelantanese women, well known for their diligence, also till the paddy and tobacco fields, barter fish on the beaches, weave brocade cloth (*songket*) and paint batik.

Left: A Kelantanese man launching an elaborately decorated moon kite. Three layers of paper cover the bamboo and rattan frame, the last comprising fine cutouts of vegetal and floral motifs. A bow attached to the kite makes a humming sound during flight. Competitions are held between groups of men whose kites are judged on their flying ability, decoration and "song".

Below right: A traditional kite maker at work. Kelantan hosts an annual kite festival, to celebrate the end of the rice harvest, at the Beach of the Seven Lagoons, a few miles north of Kota Bharu, where the experts compete to fly the biggest traditional kite. The current record is for a 9 m (30 ft) long kite.

Above and right: Hand-painted batik is one of the East Coast's specialities. The finer details of design are painted onto the cloth with wax, which stops different coloured dyes from running into each other (far right). After the wax has been removed by boiling and the excess dye washed off, the batik cloths are dried in the sun (above).

Sabah: Home to Eco Treasures

Sabah is home to some of the most amazing ecology systems on the planet. Its underwater coral reefs, uninhabited islands, extensive jungles and awesome mountains are among the most pristine in existence. This means Sabah has a big pull in the adventure and eco-tourism stakes. It has also done well at promoting itself as North Borneo, its former colonial name.

But things have not always been as upbeat for the area. Although humans have probably lived on Borneo for 37,000 years or more, the area now known as Sabah had little contact with the outside world. There was some early trade with passing Chinese vessels, but the dozens of different indigenous groups, including the famous head-hunter tribes, just got on with living in the jungle and along the coast. From the fifteenth century onwards, the Sultanate of Brunei, which lay to the south, expanded its influence and became the nominal ruler of the entire island of Borneo and beyond.

In 1658, the Sultan of Brunei gave the northeast coast of Borneo to the Sultan of Sulu in return for settling an internal war. Although this had little immediate effect on the inhabitants of the area, it is the basis for the Philippines' territorial claims here. Much later, when Sabah integrated into modern Malaysia in 1963, both the Philippines and Indonesia (which owns the eastern part of Borneo) were very hostile to the move. A minority of Sabahans still want to split with Malaysia and form a federation with Brunei and Sarawak to the south, but it seems very unlikely that such a move will ever come about.

The first European attempt to set up a base in northern Borneo occurred in 1761. That failed, and a similar attempt to turn the offshore island of Labuan into a mini Singapore from 1844 onwards was also unsuccessful. In 1882, a group of bankers based in the British port of Hong Kong leased northern Borneo as a private venture and set about organizing settlements and administering the area, following standard British colonial procedures.

Pages 86–7: A diver prepares to swim down the side of Sipidan's extinct volcanic core and investigate the remarkable coral reefs there. More than 3,000 species of fish have been logged on the Sipidan reef, making it one of the best dive sites in the world.

Above and opposite: The whimsical South Peak of Mount Kinabalu (top) is often photographed but rarely climbed, as some mountaineering experience is necessary to get to the very top. Most visitors climb instead up Low's Peak (right), which is an easier ascent, and marked by a thick white rope.

Left: Kota Kinabalu, the capital of Sabah, was basically built from scratch after the Second World War. Its modern offices and shopping centres give way to the more traditional hustle and bustle of market stalls at the seafront.

The 1942 Japanese invasion and occupation of North Borneo brought the economy to a halt. The tribes people withdrew deep into the jungle and most of the infrastructure was flattened.

After the war, North Borneo became a British colony. Sandakan, with its fantastic natural harbour but terrible wartime atrocities, was all but abandoned, and Jesselton, far away on the west coast became the new capital. Now known as Kota Kinabalu, the city is the modern gateway to Sabah.

Sabah's biggest pull is Mount Kinabalu, which was the first UNESCO World Heritage site to be declared in Malaysia. The summit is a barren, granite outcrop at 4095 metres (13,450 feet) above sea level and in order to reach it, you pass from lowland forest all the way through to alpine vegetation. Sometimes there is even snow at the top. Although the ascent is challenging, no special mountaineering equipment is required, and many visitors climb up most of the mountain on the first day, stay overnight at the Laban Rata resthouse, and then rise early in time to witness sunrise on the peak the next morning. On a good clear morning, before clouds

Above: A Rungus longhouse at the Sabah Tea Plantation in Ranau. The longhouse is one of the plantation's guesthouses and has twenty-five rooms off a communal hall.

Right: Interior of the Rungus longhouse at the Sabah Tea Plantation, showing the communal area and the separate family quarters. Modern Rungus longhouses tend to be much smaller, with around ten rooms.

Opposite: A woman in traditional costume demonstrating the use of a backstrap loom.

Pages 92–3: The limestone Gomantong Caves, set in a forest reserve near to Sandakan, are the home to more than a million swiflets. Their edible nests are harvested twice a year, using suspended rattan ladders, poles and ropes, and sold for birds' nest soup.

shroud the mountain, most of Sabah is visible.

When I climbed to the peak back in 1992, I rather congratulated myself on the speed of my ascent, until I found out about the Mount Kinabalu International Climbathon, which is an annual 21 km (13 mile) sprint up to the top of the mountain and back. It was designed to train the park rangers' rapid rescue squad for days when bad weather rules out helicopter rescues, but it now has a reputation as the world's toughest mountain race. The fastest recorded times are around two hours and 40 minutes to get all the way up and back down. It took me about four hours just to get to the top!

Sabah's other big pull is Sipidan Island, the best dive site in Malaysia. It is located off the distant southeast coast on what is Malaysia's only oceanic island, rising from an extinct volcanic core some 600 m (2,000 ft) under the sea. Ever since Jacques Cousteau visited the island in 1988 and raved about its unspoilt diversity, the island has been high on the list of best dive sites in the world. More than 3,000 species of fish and several hundred coral species have been logged in the Sipidan ecosystem.

Left and above: Semporna means "perfect" in Malay, and is an apt name for the small coastal town of Semporna in eastern Sabah. Many of its residents live in stilt villages and still enjoy a semi-nomadic life.

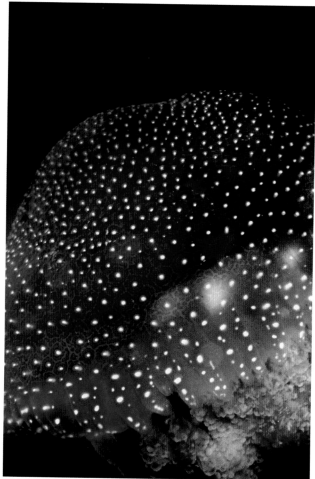

Far left and below: Turtle Island Marine Park, at the very northern tip of Sabah, is one of the world's most effective conservation programmes. Rangers protect this series of small islands, which are the hatching grounds for the graceful Green Sea Turtle (*Chelonia mydas*) (far left) and other sea turtles. Once they break out of their shells, which have been deposited in the sand, the baby turtles head back to the sea (below).

Left: Jellyfish are beautiful to look at, but can be a real hazard for divers.

Right: The landing jetty at Mabul Island, one of the places where divers can stay while visiting the Sipidan reef.

Above: Sipidan Water Village Resort on Mabul Island. This has been one of the principal upmarket resorts for Sipidan divers since 2005 when all accommodation on Sipidan Island was cleared in order to protect the area's remarkable ecosystem.

Left: The The Layang-Layang Atoll is an isolated string of thirteen coral reefs some 300 km (186 miles) north of Kota Kinabalu, where visibility is excellent and the reefs are in pristine condition.

Above: *Hypselodoris flavo-marginata*, a brightly coloured tropical sea slug found on the Sipidan reef.

Right: An ornate Ghost Pipe-fish (*Solenostomus paradoxus*) on the Sipidan reef.

Sarawak: Beyond Paradise

Sarawak, the largest of Malaysia's states, is the land of the hornbill, the orang utan and the White Rajahs. It is also home to one of the biggest caves in the world, and still retains an air of nostalgic charm, a feeling that you are entering another world. Certainly, James Brooke, who sailed into Borneo back in 1838, must have felt he was entering another world. The local Dayak tribes had revolted against their Malay rulers over forced labour in antimony mines, piracy was rampant and the deep jungle was everywhere.

Brooke helped some local leaders put down the rebellion, and by 1841 had forced the overall ruler, the Sultan of Brunei, to grant him the title of Rajah of Sarawak, a small area at the southwest of the Sultanate. Brooke then went about building his capital at Kuching on the Sarawak River, expanding his territories and establishing himself as the "White Rajah" of Sarawak. The idea of sailing halfway round the world to establish your own country seems utterly bizarre nowadays. But Brooke's arrival in Sarawak was contemporaneous with a large surge in British colonial interest in the Far East. Hong Kong was occupied in 1841 and the small island of Labuan, up the coast from Sarawak, was seized in 1840.

Brooke cut a quixotic and rather adventurous figure in his new role and took rather a paternalistic approach to his subjects as he set about reforming the administration, codifying laws and fighting piracy. He adopted the customs and pomp of the ruling Malay class and encouraged economic development through the immigration of a Chinese merchant class. The Chinese were, however, forbidden from settling outside the cities in order to preserve the way of life of the various tribes of Sarawak. Brooke encountered several rebellions during his rule, and was also summoned to London over accusations of cruelty and illegal conduct. A special commission was set up to investigate the charges, but they were never proven.

Brooke did not marry and had no direct heirs, and so he was succeeded by his nephew, Charles

Above: Built in 1879, Fort Margherita commands breathtaking views of Kuching from the north bank of the river. Named after the wife of the second White Rajah, it has now been converted into a Police Museum. The Malay village below the fort spreads out along the river in both directions.

Pages 100–1: An aerial view of Kuching ("cat" in Malay). The old town centre, built during the reign of the White Rajahs, is virtually intact, and can easily be viewed in a leisurely stroll or two. A landscaped esplanade running along the riverbank, opposite Main Bazaar, the best place to pick up local crafts, is a popular spot with both locals and visitors.

Brooke, in 1868. The third White Rajah, Charles Vyner Brooke, took over when his father died in 1917. By that time, the territory of Sarawak had expanded significantly, encircling its one-time ruler, the Sultanate of Brunei, and running all the way up to the border of another British protectorate, North Borneo.

Japan's invasion and occupation of Sarawak in 1941 marked the beginning of the end for the White Rajahs. Much of Sarawak's infrastructure was destroyed and many of the European administrative officers stationed across the country were killed. In 1946, Charles Vyner Brooke formally ceded control to the British crown. Anthony Brooke, who was the heir apparent, disputed the move. The Sarawakians were also none too happy with the turn of events and the first British governor was assassinated. But British rule went on, and in 1963 Sarawak became part of Malaysia, along with North Borneo. This sparked several years of confrontation with neighbouring Indonesia, who had demanded that the peoples of Sarawak and North Borneo be given a referendum on whether to join Malaysia or not. Tensions eventually simmered down, and bilateral

relations between Jakarta and Kuala Lumpur are now fully normalized.

For the modern visitor arriving in Kuching, the city appears as calm and serene as the slow-moving Sarawak River that flows right through it. Apart from the obvious humidity and tropical vegetation, the old centre has the unmistakable feel of a sleepy British town, with its general post office, courthouse and clock tower. On a rolling hill on the other side of the river is the Margherita Fort, which now is a Police Museum housing, amongst other things, a display of execution methods and confiscated firearms. But the most imposing structure is that of theAstana, or palace, which was home to the Brookes and is now occupied by the Governor of Sarawak.

Still, Sarawak's greatest appeal lies outside Kuching, in the jungly interior, where the biodiversity in flora and fauna is second to none, and where many of the state's indigenous people still live. A visit to a tribal longhouse is an unforgettable experience. Mostly the domain of the Iban people, the longhouses have a lengthy shared hallway and verandah, and then separate rooms for each family. Sometimes old war trophies of

human skulls still hang from the rafters, although modern radios and televisions are becoming more common sights.

The Gunung Mulu National Park in the north of Sarawak has an awesome collection of karst scenery in a mountainous rainforest setting, and well deserves its UNESCO World Heritage listing. Although only four caves are open to the public, these include the Sarawak Chamber, which was first mapped out in 1981 and is the largest known cave in the world.

I visited the park on a youth project several years ago to collect rubbish discarded by careless visitors. We were lucky enough to see several species of wildlife, probably because the food scraps in the rubbish had lured them out of their usual habitats. But generally speaking, it is quite hard to spot jungle animals in the wild. One of the only sure-fire ways of seeing some of Borneo's famous animals is to visit the Semmengoh Wildlife Rehabilitation Centre just outside Kuching. There are several orang utans here, as well as sun bears, hornbills and gibbons. For many visitors, it is the highlight of their trip to Malaysia.

Above: The Sarawak Museum has one of the best ethnological collections in Southeast Asia. The naturalist Alfred Russel Wallace, who spent two years researching the evolution of man in Sarawak, was instrumental in setting up the museum.

Left: Bamboo basketry handicrafts from Sarawak. Jungle produce has long been fashioned into items of daily use, from mats to every type of basket imaginable.

Above and right: The Sarawak Cultural Village, near to Kuching, is an excellent place to get an understanding of the diverse nature of Sarawak's peoples, and see demonstrations of traditional ways of life (above). Seven traditional dwellings, belonging to the major racial groups in Sarawak, can be explored, including the Orang Ulu longhouse (right) from central Borneo. Inside the longhouse (top) there is a collective verandah and separate apartments for each family group.

Top and right: Travelers can reach the Gunung Mulu National Park in northern Sarawak by taking a longboat along the Melinau River. Its clear waters also make for a refreshing swim.

Above: A hornbill in flight.

Opposite: The Pinnacles Limestone Forest in Gunung Mulu National Park. Some of the spikes are an impressive 45 m (148 ft) high.

Left: The Proboscis Monkey is one of Sarawak's highly endangered species.

Opposite: A traveler maneuvering a longboat out of the shallows on the Melinau River.

Above: The Orang Utan ("jungle person") is another of Sarawak's endangered species.

Top: The Rafflesia flower is the largest in the world, and can grow to diameters of more than 1 m (3 ft).

Left and right: Sarawak has an awesome collection of National Parks. The Gunung Mulu National Park (left) contains the Deer Cave (also known as the Sarawak Chamber), which is the largest known cave in the world. In the Niah National Park near the coast (right), human remains dating back an impressive 37,000 years have been excavated from what appears to be a prehistoric burial cave.

Page 112: A perfect sunset on Sabah's west coast.

建星長耀于泉有光

館會